ENGINEERING WONDERS OF THE 21ST CENTURY

Great
CAR
Designs

BY SOPHIE WASHBURNE

Cavendish
Square
NEW YORK

Published in 2023 by Cavendish Square Publishing, LLC
29 East 21st Street, New York, NY 10010

Copyright © 2023 by Cavendish Square Publishing, LLC

No part of this publication may be reproduced, stored in a retrieval system, or transmitted in any form
or by any means—electronic, mechanical, photocopying, recording, or otherwise—without the prior
permission of the copyright owner. Request for permission should be addressed to Permissions, Cavendish
Square Publishing, 29 East 21st Street, New York, NY 10010. Tel (877) 980-4450; fax (877) 980-4454.

Website: cavendishsq.com

Disclaimer: Portions of this work were originally authored by Heather Moore Niver and published
as *21st-Century Cars*. All new material this edition authored by Sophie Washburne.

This publication represents the opinions and views of the author based on his or her personal
experience, knowledge, and research. The information in this book serves as a general
guide only. The author and publisher have used their best efforts in preparing this book and
disclaim liability rising directly or indirectly from the use and application of this book.

All websites were available and accurate when this book was sent to press.

Cataloging-in-Publication Data
Names: Washburne, Sophie.
Title: Great car designs / Sophie Washburne.
Description: New York : Cavendish Square, 2023. | Series: Engineering
wonders of the 21st century | Includes glossary and index.
Identifiers: ISBN 9781502665119 (pbk.) | ISBN 9781502665133
(library bound) | ISBN 9781502665140 (ebook)
Subjects: LCSH: Automobiles--Design and construction--Juvenile literature.
| Automobiles--Technological innovations--Juvenile literature.
Classification: LCC TL240.W37 2023 | DDC 629.2'34--dc23

Editor: Jennifer Lombardo
Copyeditor: Michelle Denton
Designer: Rachel Rising

The photographs in this book are used by permission and through the courtesy of: Cover (main) Abu
hasim.A/Shutterstock.com; cover, pp. 1–48 (gears) Artistdesign29/Shutterstock.com; cover,
pp. 1–48 (grid) Cesar Termulo Jr/Shutterstock.com; cover, pp. 1–48 (boxes) Olessia_Art/
Shutterstock.com; p. 4 insidefoto srl/Alamy Stock Photo; p. 6 Eric Gevaert/Shutterstock.com; p. 7
Gorodenkoff/Shutterstock.com; p. 8 https://commons.wikimedia.org/wiki/File:Engine_of_the_
Cugnot_machine.jpg; p. 10 REUTERS/Alamy Stock Photo; p. 12 https://commons.wikimedia.org/wiki/
File:Autobus_amedee-bollee.jpg; p. 13 Farber/Shutterstock.com; p. 16 Joseph Sohm/Shutterstock.com;
p. 18 ssuaphotos/Shutterstock.com; p. 20 https://commons.m.wikimedia.org/wiki/File:Morrison_
vehicle_undercarriage_motor.jpg; p. 25 VectorMine/Shutterstock.com; p. 26 Dan74/Shutterstock.com;
p. 28 Steve Lagreca/Shutterstock.com; p. 31 lidiasilva/Shutterstock.com; p. 33 Flystock/Shutterstock.
com; p. 36 sdecoret/Shutterstock.com; p. 38 dpa picture alliance/Alamy Stock Photo; p. 39 Iaremenko
Sergii/Shutterstock.com; p. 40 Chinnapong/Shutterstock.com; p. 42 Aflo Co. Ltd./Alamy Stock Photo.

Some of the images in this book illustrate individuals who are models.
The depictions do not imply actual situations or events.

CPSIA compliance information: Batch #CSCSQ23: For further information contact
Cavendish Square Publishing LLC, New York, New York, at 1-877-980-4450.

Printed in the United States of America

Find us on

CONTENTS

Introduction

The invention of the automobile, or car, changed transportation forever. During the time of the Roman Empire, the fastest carriages available took often days or even weeks to get people where they needed to go because they were pulled by animals. Today, thanks to cars, long journeys often only take hours instead. Faster transportation gives people more time to do other things and makes it easier for people to travel.

This model is based on Leonardo da Vinci's drawing of a mechanical cart.

People did not stop once they invented the automobile. Today, engineers are always looking for ways to make cars faster, safer, and more **efficient**. They also want to solve other issues that have come about as cars have changed over the years.

The famous artist and inventor Leonardo da Vinci is considered to have drawn the first versions of many inventions, including the car. Around 1478, he drew a sketch of a mechanical cart that was not pulled by horses. It was the first known design in history for a vehicle that would move on its own, and it was incredibly complex. In fact, experts say it was so complex that it could never have been built during Leonardo's lifetime. The tools needed to make the parts simply did not exist yet. However, that does not mean the vehicle would not have worked. In 2004, a team of engineers succeeded in building a small model of the self-propelled cart according to Leonardo's design. It uses springs, so it needs to be wound up before it can move. Every time it stops, it needs to be wound again. It would not be a practical way to travel today, but it was an amazing idea for its time period.

Leonardo da Vinci was not the only person to think of ways to improve travel. By 1500, the Chinese were traveling in chariots propelled by the wind. Around 1602, a Dutch scientist

Land yachts run best on sand, which is why races mainly take place on beaches or in deserts.

named Simon Stevin built something similar. Today, this type of car is known as a land **yacht**, and it has been redesigned to be faster and lighter over the years. It is used mainly for racing, not for transportation.

Cars have gone through many design changes over the years with the arrival of new technology and new information. Today, they are more **aerodynamic**, safer, and technologically advanced. Engineers are working all the time to make cars better and more interesting. There are even plans for flying cars! No one knows for sure what the future of automobiles will look like, but one thing is certain: It will definitely be exciting.

Today, engineers use computer-aided design (CAD) to solve problems before a car is actually built.

Nicolas-Joseph Cugnot's horseless carriage engine had a huge boiler (*shown here*) because it ran on steam power.

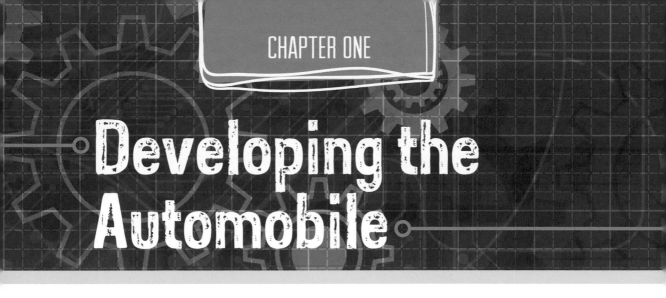

CHAPTER ONE

Developing the Automobile

The invention of the car was not just one moment in history. Long before the technology to build vehicles was available, people were dreaming them up and describing how they might work. Sometimes people were able to build these things years later, when technology had caught up with their ideas.

USING STEAM POWER

Before anything resembling the car as we now know it came to be, there was the carriage. At first, inventors simply adapted horse carts to work with engines, so the early models were called "horseless carriages." In 1769, Nicolas-Joseph Cugnot built the world's first full-size, self-propelled vehicle. It rolled around on three wheels and was powered by steam. Cugnot made it for moving pieces of artillery, or weapons. Although the automobile worked, it could run for only 20 minutes at

2.25 miles (3.6 kilometers) per hour; then it needed to stop to build up a fresh supply of steam. Cugnot used descriptions of a theoretical steam engine that were written in 1679 by a French physicist named Dennis Papin. Steam carriages continued to be developed in the 18th and 19th centuries, including one in the United States in 1805, which was designed by Oliver Evans. His car was amphibious, meaning it worked both on land and in the water. Evans built it to clear garbage and other debris from the Philadelphia, Pennsylvania, waterfront.

Shown here are examples of more modern amphibious vehicles.

An Idea That Never Caught On

Although we have had the ability to make amphibious cars since the early 1800s, they are not common. During World War II (1939–1945), both Germany and the United States made amphibious vehicles. After the war, the American ones, which were called "the ducks," were sold off. A man named Mel Flath bought some of them and started a sightseeing company called Duck Tours. People can still book these tours today in some cities.

In the 1960s, an amphibious vehicle called the Amphicar was marketed to everyday Americans. Although it worked, it was made of steel, which rusts easily. Within 10 years, most of these cars were unusable, although some have been restored by collectors. By 1989, car manufacturers were able to use lightweight, rustproof materials. However, because of the way the car was shaped, it could not go faster than around 6 miles (10 km) per hour in the water. Some companies have redesigned their amphibious cars; for example, the Watercar can **retract** its wheels to achieve speeds of up to 60 miles (96 km) per hour in the water. However, amphibious cars are more expensive than regular cars. Few people can afford them, and people who do not live near water have no use for them.

Throughout most of the rest of the 1800s, people focused on improving steam technology and car safety. They invented things such as brakes, better ways of steering, and engines that could go faster and run for longer periods of time. Most of the cars that were invented around this time were **prototypes** and

Amédée Bollée's first car (*shown here*) could carry up to 12 passengers.

were never put into large-scale production. The first car to be made in large numbers was designed by a Frenchman named Amédée Bollée. It could go as fast as 25 miles (40 km) per hour. Bollée built one for his personal use in 1873, and it went into production in 1878.

A BETTER ENGINE

In the 1860s, a Belgian inventor named Étienne Lenoir designed and built the first successful internal combustion engine, which ran on coal gas. "Combustion" means burning and "internal" means inside, so the name gives a general idea of how the engine works: It burns fuel inside itself. Internal combustion engines have cylinders in them. Each cylinder has a moving part called a piston attached to it. Valves on the cylinder let fuel in and **emissions** out. The emissions a car lets off are called exhaust. Each cylinder also has a part called a spark plug, which ignites the fuel.

As an engine runs, it goes through several strokes, or phases. Most car engines have four strokes: intake, compression, combustion, and exhaustion. On the intake stroke, the valve at the top opens to let fuel and air into the cylinder. On the compression stroke, the valve closes, and the piston moves to the top. As it goes up, its movement compresses, or squeezes, the fuel and air into a small space. In the combustion stroke, the

This diagram illustrates how a four-stroke combustion engine works.

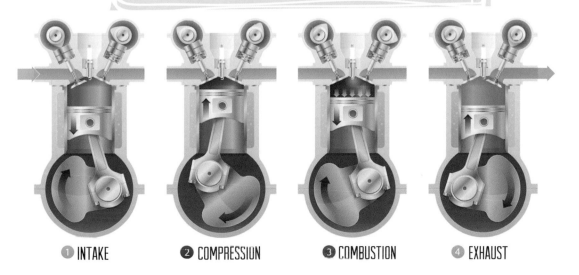

① INTAKE   ② COMPRESSIUN   ③ COMBUSTION   ④ EXHAUST

spark plug ignites the fuel, creating a small explosion that forces the piston back down. On the exhaust stroke, a different valve opens, and the piston rises up again to push out the exhaust from the burned fuel. The parts of the engine are connected, so the piston's movement causes the rest of the parts of the engine to move. The invention of an effective internal combustion engine was an essential step toward the production of modern cars. In 1862, Lenoir built a version of his engine that could run on liquid fuel and used it to power a car he had built. This was the first car to use an internal combustion engine. It took between 2 and 3 hours to make a 6-mile (10 km) trip.

In 1876, German engineer Nikolaus Otto and his business partner, Eugen Langen, improved on Lenoir's design. Lenoir's engine had only two strokes, so some of the engine's functions happened at the same time. Otto and Langen gave Lenoir's engine two more strokes, which made it more efficient. Less fuel was needed to power the engine, and less was lost during the exhaustion stroke. They also designed it to run on gasoline. Their engine became known as the Otto cycle engine, and the term "Otto cycle" now refers to all compressed charge, four-cycle engines.

By 1885, the public was able to buy gasoline-fueled automobiles. Karl Benz of Mannheim, Germany, offered the

Motorwagen, which had three wheels and reached speeds of 6 miles (10 km) per hour—about the same as a brisk walking pace. However, to his dismay, nobody seemed interested in buying it. At the time, many people viewed cars with distrust. At best, they seemed like something fun but not very useful, so many people did not want to waste their money on one.

MAKING MORE IMPROVEMENTS

In 1885, a German man named Gottlieb Daimler and his design partner, Wilhelm Maybach, improved on Otto's internal combustion engine, creating what is now widely considered the model for the gas engine that is most commonly used today. This new engine was revolutionary for its small, light design, as well as for its efficiency. On March 8, 1886, Daimler created a four-wheeled automobile by adapting a stagecoach to hold the engine.

In 1889, Daimler and Maybach took things a step further: Instead of fitting an engine into an existing vehicle, they built their entire structure. This automobile boasted a four-speed **transmission** and could motor along at speeds up to 10 miles (16 km) per hour. The next year, Daimler established Daimler Motoren-Gesellschaft, where he could build his creations. Maybach went on to create the Mercedes in 1901.

The early 1900s effectively marked the beginning of the automobile industry, as these new, faster cars began to seem useful. Car dealerships began to open, and people began to hold auto shows so the public could see the new technology. These were a big part of getting people interested in buying cars. Manufacturers demonstrated how the cars could steer, brake, turn, climb hills, and more. People who did not believe a car could replace horses saw for themselves that they were wrong.

The Ford Model T (*shown here*) is one of the world's most famous cars. Like all cars produced before electric starters became standard in 1920, the engine was started with a hand crank on the front of the car.

As the demand for cars increased, Ransom E. Olds saw that they needed to be produced faster and in larger numbers. Although Henry Ford is often credited with creating the assembly line, it was the Oldsmobile that was the first car to be mass-produced, starting in 1901. Ford's company, General Motors, bought Oldsmobile in 1908, and the company continued to produce Oldsmobiles until 2004. Ford improved the assembly process around 1914 by installing a conveyor belt, which significantly reduced the time it took to assemble an automobile.

Cars have only increased in popularity over the years. Not only are they a practical way to get around, they have also become a hobby for many people. Car lovers go to auto shows and talk about the designs they like. For people who simply want to get from point A to point B easily, engineers are working all the time to make cars faster, more efficient, and safer.

THINK IT THROUGH

1. Why do you think boats and cars need to be shaped differently to move efficiently?
2. Why do you think Henry Ford often gets the most credit when discussing the history of the automobile?
3. Why do you think many people in the late 1800s distrusted cars?

Because catalytic converters change most of a car's dangerous chemicals into water, we can see the water vapor coming out of the exhaust pipe on cold days. Many people confuse this water vapor for harmful smoke.

CHAPTER TWO

An Environmental Problem

So many people rely on cars today that it is certain they are not going to disappear any time soon. However, we now know that they cause a lot of problems for the environment. For one thing, their emissions are a big cause of climate change. For another, the gas and oil they need to run are not renewable resources. At some point, if people do not figure out a different way to make cars work efficiently, we will run out of these resources. Thankfully, engineers are already hard at work on this issue.

IMPROVED EFFICIENCY

Improving the efficiency of a car has multiple benefits. It lets the car run for longer on one tank of fuel. Filling up less often saves car owners money. It also decreases the amount of exhaust that is released. Some ways to make an engine more efficient are to makc it run hotter, push more air into it during the intake stroke, or make it easier for the exhaust to leave the engine. However, there is a limit to how efficient an engine can be because it will always produce some kind of waste as a result of the work it is doing.

Only about 56 percent of the energy stored in gasoline can theoretically be converted in a useful way by an engine. The rest is turned into heat, which does not help an engine run better. However, in reality, engines are only about 40 percent efficient. This is because it is impossible to create engine parts that work perfectly all the time. Engines wear down with use, and parts need to be replaced. In 1973, engineers created the catalytic converter to try to address the emissions problem. This device is attached to a car's exhaust system to convert the very dangerous gases a car produces, such as carbon monoxide and hydrocarbons, into less dangerous ones, such as carbon dioxide and water. Carbon monoxide can be deadly, and hydrocarbons

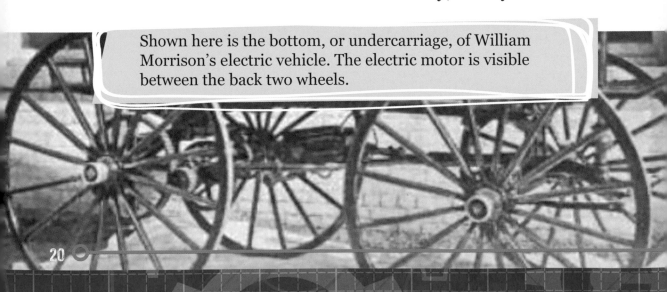

Shown here is the bottom, or undercarriage, of William Morrison's electric vehicle. The electric motor is visible between the back two wheels.

create smog when they are released into the air. Therefore, the converters made the air at the street level cleaner. However, carbon dioxide is still causing climate change. To make a big difference, engineers had to look at how to redesign an engine to not need gasoline at all.

LOOKING BACK AT ELECTRIC

Many people think of electric cars as new technology, but in fact, people started experimenting with them in 1830! In 1891, William Morrison began producing the first electric cars in the United States. More than 50 other manufacturers started to produce them too. The electric cars at this time could go about 20 miles (32 km) per hour, and their batteries needed to be recharged after about 50 miles (80 km). At the time, this was much further and faster than a gas-powered car could go, and the ride was smoother and cleaner as well. However, as people improved the internal combustion engine, it soon became the much more popular—not to mention cheaper—choice.

Electric vehicles became a technology of interest again after a gas shortage in the 1970s. However, an internal combustion engine can only work with liquid fuel, so engineers had to take a look at the engine design. Unlike an internal combustion engine, an electric engine has very few moving parts. The battery creates a magnetic force that spins a part in the engine called the rotor. When the rotor spins, it creates the energy that turns the car's wheels.

IT'S ELECTRIC!

Today, electric cars are becoming very popular. They are more expensive to buy, but they are cheaper to maintain. They also produce fewer emissions than gas, which is better for the environment, and they are more efficient. However, they still have some problems that need to be solved before more people buy them. For example, electric cars need to be charged every so often. Some places have charging stations that are similar to gas stations. However, these are not very common, so it can be difficult to go far in an electric car.

One way engineers have gotten around this problem is by making **hybrid** cars. Hybrids combine an extremely efficient gas engine with a battery system or electric motor. Advanced electronics in the engine and transmission controls adjust the engine according to the type of driving a person is doing. For example, some car engines shut off when the car is stopped and restart again when the brake pedal is lifted. This saves fuel in places with slow-moving traffic, such as a traffic jam. Hybrid cars also remove the need for charging stations because the car becomes its own battery charger as it drives.

Issues with Electric Cars

Many people believe switching to electric cars can save the environment. However, the answer is not so simple. It is true that electric cars produce fewer emissions while driving than gas-powered cars. However, the process of making the battery produces more emissions than making a car does. Furthermore, the power grid in most American cities is powered by fossil fuels. This means that charging an electric car still uses gas, oil, and coal. Many experts say electric cars will not truly be better for the environment until the United States uses more renewable energy sources, such as wind and solar power, for its power grids. However, they also say that right now, electric cars are still better than gas-powered cars.

Another problem is the way batteries are made. Most batteries are made with a metal called lithium, which needs to be mined, or dug out of the ground. Lithium mining is very bad for the environment and has caused many animal deaths. It also wastes a lot of water, which has caused a shortage in the nation of Chile. To address this problem, some scientists are trying to figure out how to make batteries that do not run on lithium. However, as of 2021, they are a long way from a good solution.

OTHER KINDS OF FUEL

Some car manufacturers are working on making their cars run on fuels that are cleaner and more sustainable. No alternative fuel that has been developed as of 2021 is as efficient as gasoline, which means a car that ran on one of them would need to be refueled much more often. This is why alternative fuels are mixed with gasoline instead of replacing it completely.

Ethyl alcohol, better known as ethanol, is one of the most common alternative fuels. This renewable resource is easily made from plant sources such as corn and sugarcane. The most common blend of gasoline and ethanol, which is called gasohol, uses 10 percent ethanol. Any engine can use this blend. Some cars with specially designed engines can also use a blend that is up to 85 percent ethanol. Methanol is another gas alternative. Also known as methyl alcohol or wood alcohol, methanol is extracted from wood products or, more efficiently, from natural gas.

Methanol has several positive features that make it a good use for fuel. It is inexpensive to produce compared to other non-gasoline fuels. It is also safer to use because it is not as flammable as gasoline. However, many people worry about its impact on the environment. Natural gas is easiest to come by through a process called **fracking**. This process creates a lot of wastewater, which pollutes areas near where it occurs. Another problem with using methanol as a main fuel source is that pure methanol can damage a car's fuel lines if it stays in them for too long. A methanol-gasoline mixture is often used in the car racing industry because it creates more power and works well for boosting engines, but for people who do not need that kind of speed boost, it appears to have more drawbacks than advantages.

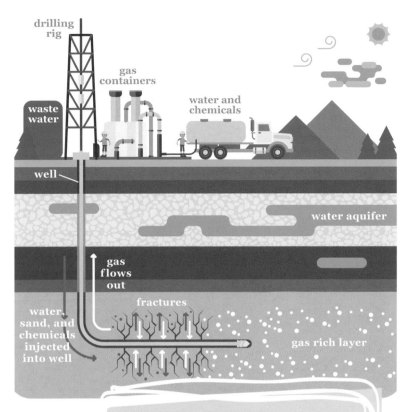

drilling
rig

gas
containers

water and
chemicals

waste
water

well

water aquifer

gas
flows
out

water,
sand, and
chemicals
injected
into well

fractures

gas rich layer

THINK IT THROUGH

This diagram shows how fracking works. Because the drill needs to go through the groundwater layer to get to the gas layer, it pollutes the water at drill sites.

1. Why would making an engine run hotter increase its efficiency?

2. Why do you think many people are still hesitant to buy electric vehicles?

3. Can you think of any other changes that could be made to create cars that are better for the environment?

Some cars are not mass-produced the way most are. Since so few are made, these cars are hard to find, which adds to their value. The Ferrari 250 GTO (*shown here*) is one such car.

CHAPTER THREE

A Symbiotic Relationship

Over the years, people and cars have developed a kind of symbiotic relationship—where both things work together. For some people, learning about cars is a hobby. Different people have different ideas about what makes a car look good. Some people like antique cars, such as the Ford Model T. Other people like classic cars, such as thc Ferrari 250 GTO. Still others prefer new, sleek cars, such as the Lamborghini Veneno. However, most cars are made to do the work of simply transporting people from one place to another. The manufacturers of these cars focus more on safety than looks.

COOL CARS

Some car manufacturers partner with car design houses, or companies, to make unique styles. Five of the most famous and respected design houses are Pininfarina, Zagato, Bertone, Italdesign Giugiaro, and Carrozzeria Ghia.

Porsche is a car maker that is best known for sports cars and race cars. One of the best modern sports cars it has made is a model called the Cayman. Porsche announced in 2021 that the 2025 Cayman 718 will be the manufacturer's most modern car ever. It will be fully electric, and it will be made of lightweight materials. The lighter a car is, the faster it can go, the better its **handling** is, and the easier it can stop.

Many car enthusiasts love a fast car, and Chevrolet's Corvette is at the top of many lists, with models for the highway

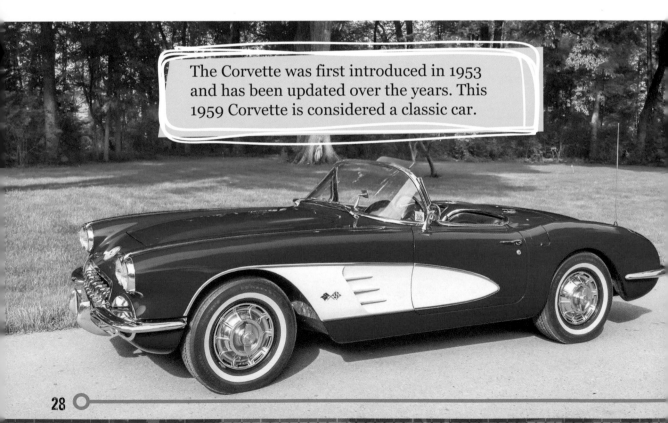

The Corvette was first introduced in 1953 and has been updated over the years. This 1959 Corvette is considered a classic car.

The Need for Speed

Car racing is a huge pastime for many people. There are multiple kinds of races, including stock car, rally car, and sports car. Each race uses a different kind of car. For example, Formula 1 (F1) racers drive a single-seat, open-cockpit racing car. Its engine is behind the driver, not in the front of the car. IndyCars, which are driven in the Indianapolis 500 race, look very similar, but they are shorter and lighter than F1 cars. Many sports cars and race cars perform better than ever thanks to high-tech materials. Graphene, for example, is a kind of carbon that is considered a "wonder material" because even though it is thin and light, it is 200 times stronger than steel.

NASCAR cars look quite different than F1 and IndyCars. They look more like regular cars, but they can achieve speeds and make turns that a car such as an everyday Dodge or Ford can never match. To improve the car's handling, its weight is distributed more evenly over the axles of the wheels by putting the engine and the transmission—the heaviest parts of the car—as close to the middle of the car as possible. This does not leave a lot of room in the car for passengers or cargo, which is why regular cars are not designed this way.

and for racing around the track. The C7, known as the Stingray, was a convertible released in 2017. For those with a need for speed, the Stingray can help make the driving experience even better. A review in *Consumer Reports* mentioned the car's quick acceleration, smooth handling, and fantastic looks. It has eight speeds, compared to the six offered in the 2015 model.

In addition, a Performance Data Recorder can record video of a driving session and offer real-time data during the drive. It can all be saved to a memory card to review later so someone can learn how to improve their driving.

REMOVING HUMAN ERROR

While speed and looks are often the top concerns for concept cars and race cars, the main thing the manufacturers of most cars keep in mind is safety. One thing many people believe would make cars safer is if they drove themselves. Humans can cause car crashes by getting distracted, falling asleep, or not reacting fast enough. A machine does not have these problems. Fully autonomous, or self-driving, cars are still in development. However, many cars have safety features that involve letting the machine do some of the work. There are six levels of driving automation:

• **Level 0:** Manual cars that use a **clutch** to change gears are Level 0 cars.

• **Level 1:** Cars that can shift gears automatically and have very simple features to make driving easier, such as cruise control, are Level 1.

- **Level 2:** Cars that can control steering as well as speed are Level 2. Drivers still need to pay close attention and make driving decisions.

- **Level 3:** Similarly to Level 2, these cars can control steering and speed. They also take input from their surroundings to make driving decisions in limited situations, such as speeding up to pass a slower car. Drivers still need to pay attention most of the time and be ready to take over in a situation the car cannot control.

In a manual car, which is Level 0, there is an extra pedal called the clutch (*far right*). Drivers have to hold this down while they shift gears or else the gears will grind against each other, which is bad for the engine.

- **Level 4:** Cars that can make all the driving decisions and do not need a human to take over in most circumstances are Level 4. Very few of these exist, and they have to stay in certain areas. They are mainly used for public transportation.
- **Level 5:** As of 2021, there are very few Level 5 cars. They can do everything by themselves, so riders do not need to pay attention at all.

In 2017, Audi announced that its A8 would have a Level 3 program called Traffic Jam Assist that allows the car to accelerate, brake, and steer on its own. This can only happen on divided highways when the car is in traffic going less than 37 miles (60 km) per hour, and the car is not able to change lanes on its own. The car warns the driver when they need to take over again, so although someone's attention can wander a bit, they cannot fall asleep. Audi has no plans as of 2021 to offer it in the United States.

Tesla is another company that is working on giving cars more driving control. It offers a Level 2 feature called Autopilot, which allows the car to make its way through traffic using a camera, radar on the bumper, and special sensors on the front and rear. In 2021, Ford also released a Level 2 technology called BlueCruise on two of its cars. Drivers do not need to have their hands on the wheel all the time, but the car has a camera that watches the driver to make sure they are ready to take over at a moment's notice. Ford is also working on technology that will let their cars change lanes by themselves when the turn signal is activated.

A WAYS TO GO

Companies have been promising that self-driving cars are just a couple years away for a long time now, and in some cases, this is true. Companies such as Waymo by Google are testing out their Level 5 cars, and some farming and mining companies

In a Level 4 car, a person can relax and concentrate on things other than the road unless the car prompts them to take over.

use vehicles with Level 4 or 5 technology. However, we are still a long way from replacing all cars with self-driving ones.

There are many problems that still need to be solved because humans can do many things machines, even advanced ones, cannot. For example, a self-driving car would use sensors to figure out things such as where to turn, when to speed up, and when to swerve to avoid a sudden obstacle such as an animal in the road. However, machine sensors are very delicate and often do not work as well in very low or very high temperatures. Additionally, a camera on the outside of a vehicle could be covered by blowing snow or leaves, leaving the car unable to drive. Many computer programs that currently exist are also having trouble telling the difference between things such as a flock of birds and a bunch of leaves blowing into the road. A human driver would know to stop for the birds and drive through the leaves, but a computer gets confused.

Many people believe self-driving cars cannot safely be used on the road until every car is self-driving. For instance, if a car did stop suddenly on the highway because it confused blowing leaves for birds, it could cause a crash because the human drivers behind it would not be expecting it and would likely not stop fast enough. Some Tesla and Mazda cars have been recalled because of this exact problem. Engineers are currently working on a system that scans road maps to give the car a picture of what is around it; for instance, this is how Ford's BlueCruise operates. However, for a fully autonomous car, problems can arise if something ends up on the road that is not on the map. This also limits where the cars can drive; anywhere that has not been mapped would be impossible for the car to navigate.

There are many questions that still need to be answered: How much would a ride in a self-driving car cost? Where would the car go when it is not in use? How will people get to places that have not been mapped yet? Will people be stranded on the highway if the road changes but the map does not update? What happens if the car takes a wrong turn or the passenger changes their mind about where they want to go? Engineers are working on all of these problems, but until they solve them all perfectly, a world full of self-driving cars will remain a dream.

THINK IT THROUGH

1. What kind of design do you think makes a car beautiful?

2. Do you think self-driving cars are too dangerous to use? Why or why not?

3. What are some ways engineers can solve the problems self-driving cars still have?

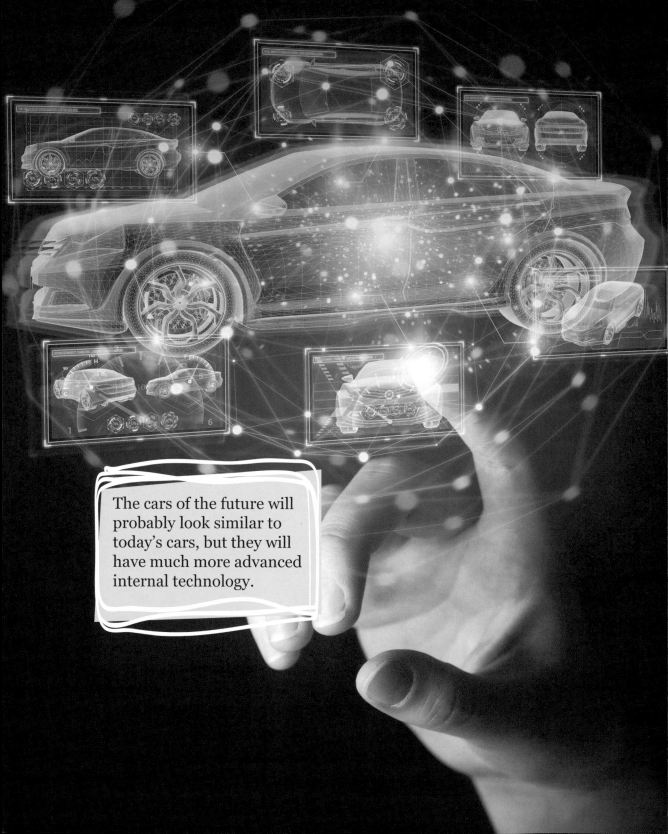

The cars of the future will probably look similar to today's cars, but they will have much more advanced internal technology.

CHAPTER FOUR

What's Next?

Engineers are hard at work on ways to make cars safer, faster, and more interesting. Some of the most exciting cars are concept cars, which are made to show off new ideas and technology—often technology that is not going to be available until far into the future.

For example, in 2021, Audi revealed a concept car called the Grandsphere. It is designed for a future in which Level 5 automation has been perfected. For this reason, its steering wheel and pedals fold into the floor when the car is in self-driving mode, leaving more leg room for the passengers. The large dashboard has a projector in it. When a human is driving, the fuel and speed gauges are projected onto it. In self-driving mode, passengers can project movies to watch or books to read. It also has two small electric engines, one for the front wheels and one for the back. The Grandsphere, like most concept cars, will likely never be put into production, since the technology to make it work is still being perfected as of 2021.

INVENTIONS FOR SAFETY AND COMFORT

One thing engineers are working on is using **biometrics** in cars. This can help with both security and safety. For example, unlocking the car with a fingerprint instead of a key could help prevent theft. Additionally, biometrics could let the car pay attention to the driver. If they fall asleep at the wheel, sensors could note it and let the car take over. The car might pull off the road and turn off, for example. Other sensors might note if the driver is showing signs of nodding off and trigger a warning to alert them. A car could monitor breathing and heart rate, too, and take control if the driver falls unconscious or has a medical emergency such as a heart attack. Some designs might help

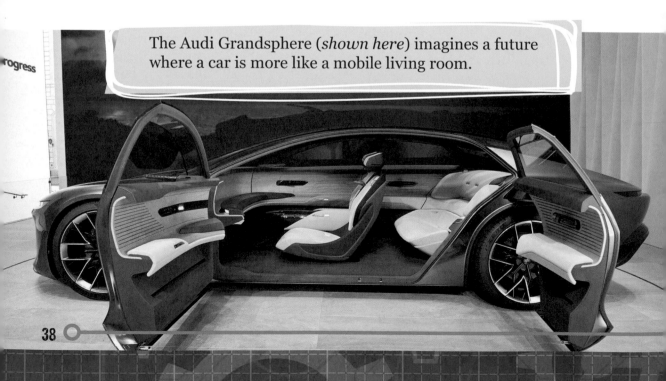

The Audi Grandsphere (*shown here*) imagines a future where a car is more like a mobile living room.

Airless tires could arrange their spokes in many different ways. Michelin's tire looks like the one to the front and right of this photo.

the car sense when an accident is about to happen and adjust things in the car for safety, such as closing windows or moving the seat back so the driver does not fly through the windshield or break their ribs on the steering wheel.

Another **innovation** that could make cars safer as well as more convenient is airless tires. The tire manufacturer Michelin promises to have airless tires on the market by 2024. The wheels feature plastic spokes around a rubber rim. The spokes bend as the tire encounters different kinds of road conditions. An airless tire means no one would ever have to change a flat tire, check their tire pressure, or worry about a **blowout**—an occurrence that causes thousands of crashes each year.

An app called CarPlay lets a person's car act like their phone.

Engineers are also working on options that focus on comfort. Volkswagen (VW) introduced a concept van in 2017 that features a **reconfigurable** interior. This could make it easier for passengers in the back seat to talk to each other, play games on long drives, or take a nap. Additionally, many cars already have the ability to connect to a driver's phone. This lets the car act as a sort of personal assistant for the driver. Phone calls can play through the car's speakers, and addresses can be plugged into the car's built-in global positioning system (GPS). Engineers hope to improve this feature in the future.

FLYING CARS

Anyone who has ever watched or read science fiction has probably thought about flying cars. Engineers are hard at

A Car Made from Plants

In 2019, a concept car called the Nano Cellulose Vehicle (NCV) was brought to the motor show in Tokyo, Japan. Its production was suggested by the Japanese Ministry of the Environment and made with the combined effort of 22 Japanese companies and universities. The NCV is made from a plant material called nanocellulose, which is lighter than steel but five times as strong. It can be used instead of metal, plastic, and glass. Furthermore, unlike a car made of steel and plastic, the NCV can be recycled when it reaches the end of its usefulness.

While it is unlikely that cars will be made completely from nanocellulose any time soon, researchers were expected to start using it in certain car parts starting in 2020. The lightness of the material will make the car handle better, go faster, and use fuel more efficiently. This makes it not only better for the environment, but also more fun for car lovers to drive.

work on some promising options. A Japanese company called SkyDrive is testing its vertical takeoff and landing (VTOL) car, and a Slovakian company called AeroMobil has a prototype for a car that can take off like a plane from a runway. Many flying car concepts look more like private helicopters than cars, and the idea is that people will use them for ridesharing. In other words, instead of getting an Uber of Lyft driver to come to your house, someday you might be able to have a flying vehicle land on your street instead!

Other flying cars can transition from driving on the road to flying in the air. One such car is the Aska, which is made by an Israeli/American company called NFT. It has rotors, or rotating blades, that can fold up when the car is in driving mode and unfold to helicopter size when it is time to fly. As a car, it will only be able to get up to 70 miles (112 km) per hour, but in the air, the company promises speeds up to 250 miles (402 km) per hour. As of 2021, this car is still only a concept.

In 2020, SkyDrive showed a model of its flying car at an exhibition in Tokyo.

As with self-driving cars, many problems still need to be solved before we can have flying cars. For example, the thing that keeps airplanes from crashing into each other is their connection to a person at air traffic control. This would be impossible with hundreds of flying vehicles, so the cars would need to be able to communicate with each other electronically and be either partially or fully autonomous. People will also likely need a pilot's license in addition to a driver's license to use any of the cars that are being designed. Flying cars will also be incredibly expensive—up to $1 million! For now, most people will have to be content with the amazing advancements that are taking place on the ground.

THINK IT THROUGH

1. What cool things would you like to see in a concept car?
2. Aside from eliminating blowouts, how can airless tires improve safety?
3. What do engineers need to consider when designing a car that can both drive on the road and fly in the sky?

GLOSSARY

aerodynamic: Relating to the qualities of an object that affect how easily it moves through the air.

biometrics: Dealing with data related to living things.

blowout: A form of tire failure in which the tire explodes due to a combination of high pressure and a sudden loss of air from a weak spot in the tire.

clutch: The pedal that operates a vehicle's clutch, which connects or disconnects with a car's transmission system.

efficient: Able to produce a desired result with little waste.

emissions: Substances that are discharged into the air.

fracking: The process of injecting liquid into rock to extract gas.

handling: In cars, the ability to make tight turns smoothly at high speeds.

hybrid: An object that is a combination of two or more different things.

innovation: A new and original idea.

prototype: An original or first model of something from which other forms are copied.

reconfigurable: Able to be changed around.

retract: To pull something back into something larger that covers it.

transmission: A system in an automobile that moves power from the engine to the wheels.

yacht: A large boat that is used for racing or pleasure.

FIND OUT MORE

Books

Chandler, Matt. *The Tech Behind Electric Cars*. North Mankato, MN: Capstone Press, 2020.

Gish, Ashley. *Sports Cars*. Mankato, MN: Creative Education, 2021.

Storey, Rita. *How To Build Cars*. London, UK: Franklin Watts, 2018.

Websites

BrainPOP: Cars
www.brainpop.com/technology/ transportation/cars
Watch movies, take quizzes, and play games to learn about how cars work.

DK Find Out: History of Cars
www.dkfindout.com/us/ transportation/history-cars
Read about the development of many kinds of cars throughout history.

History: Automobile History
www.history.com/topics/automobiles
Check out the development of cars, from Henry Ford's first model to today's cutting-edge marvels.

Organizations

Cardaddy.org
2733 North Power Road
Suite 102, PMB 174
Mesa, AZ 85215
Email: info@cardaddy.org
cardaddy.org
This organization connects car-loving children who are battling cancer and other terminal illnesses with the owners of classic or rare cars.

Classic Car Club of America
3501 Algonquin Road
Suite 300
Rolling Meadows, IL 60008
Email: info@classiccarclub.org
www.classiccarclub.org
This organization connects fans of classic cars through national events. It also publishes information about the technology and history of classic cars.

Petersen Automotive Museum
6060 Wiltshire Boulevard
Los Angeles, CA 90036
Email: info@petersen.org
www.petersen.org
This museum has many different kinds of cars on display as well as rotating exhibits on different topics, such as the cars from James Bond movies and the future of electric vehicles.

Publisher's note to educators and parents: Our editors have carefully reviewed these websites to ensure that they are suitable for students. Many websites change frequently, however, and we cannot guarantee that a site's future contents will continue to meet our high standards of quality and educational value. Be advised that students should be closely supervised whenever they access the Internet.

INDEX